The New Forest

Anne-Marie Edwards

COUNTRYSIDE BOOKS
NEWBURY BERKSHIRE

First Published 2007
© Anne-Marie Edwards, 2007
Reprinted 2011, 2013
Revised and updated 2016

All rights reserved. No reproduction
permitted without the prior permission
of the publisher:

COUNTRYSIDE BOOKS
3 Catherine Road
Newbury, Berkshire

To view our complete range of books,
please visit us at
www.countrysidebooks.co.uk

ISBN 978 1 84674 020 6

Cover picture of the New Forest
supplied by Mike Edwards

Maps by Gelder Design & Mapping

Designed by Peter Davies, Nautilus Design
Produced through The Letterworks Ltd, Reading
Printed by The Holywell Press, Oxford

Contents

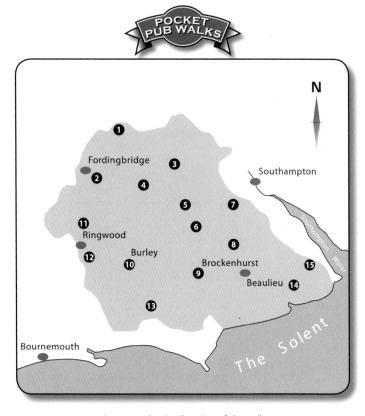

POCKET PUB WALKS

N

❶

Fordingbridge   ❸

❷   Southampton

❹

❺   ❼

❻

⓫

Ringwood   ❽

⓬   Burley

⓮   ⓯   Brockenhurst

⓾   ❾

Beaulieu   ⓮

⓭

Bournemouth

The Solent

Southampton Water

Area map showing location of the walks

Introduction

This is my sixth book of walks in the New Forest and I think it is time I offered you something a little different! When William the Conqueror, in 1079, decided he would like a hunting forest close to his capital at Winchester the thought that he would be displacing a few Saxons in the process never crossed his mind. He put a large area of southern England under Forest law, which meant that it became his own preserve and no one would be able to farm it. His New Forest covered much more countryside than the Forest of today. It reached north into Wiltshire, west over the Avon valley, south to the Solent and east to the shores of Southampton Water. Naturally, with the years, the Forest area decreased in size as surrounding towns and villages expanded. Parts of the Forest, such as the Exbury, Beaulieu and Rothschild estates, passed into private hands. The boundaries of the recently created National Park have confined its limits even further. A great deal of beautiful and historic countryside that has been part of the Forest's story for hundreds of years is now excluded. So I have decided to join William the Conqueror and write a book of walks within boundaries he would recognise!

I have included some walks from my favourite villages within the National Park. These include rambles from Minstead to discover Furzey Gardens, from Fritham to the shore of Eyeworth Pond, from Lyndhurst to enjoy views far over the Forest's loveliest woodlands, and from Brockenhurst across heaths threaded with streams. But there are also splendid walks beyond its boundaries. For example, you will find a delightful walk around Woodfalls where fine beech and oak woods sweep down to the Avon valley. Another ramble south of Fawley leads through remote countryside to a beautiful lake covered in white waterlilies and there is an interesting walk to Exbury following the mysterious Dark Water valley.

All the walks are circular and are between 2½ and 5 miles in length, and I have included details of how to get to the starting point and where to park. And, combined with your walk, what could be better than a visit to a good pub with the promise of a warm welcome, a tasty meal and a refreshing drink? The pubs in this book differ widely but I have enjoyed my visits to all of them and I think you will too. When walks start from pub car parks the owners and licensees have said that they are happy for customers to leave their cars there while walking, but have a word with them first. And it is a good idea to telephone ahead if you plan to arrive before opening time.

I have enjoyed writing this book of walks very much. Happy walking in the Conqueror's New Forest!

Anne-Marie Edwards

Publisher's Note

We hope that you obtain considerable enjoyment from this book; great care has been taken in its preparation. However, changes of landlord and actual closures are sadly not uncommon. Likewise, although at the time of publication all routes followed public rights of way or permitted paths, diversion orders can be made and permissions withdrawn.

We cannot, of course, be held responsible for such diversion orders and any inaccuracies in the text which result from these or any other changes to the routes nor any damage which might result from walkers trespassing on private property. We are anxious though that all details covering the walks and pubs are kept up to date and would therefore welcome information from readers which would be relevant to future editions.

The simple sketch maps that accompany the walks in this book are based on notes made by the author whilst checking out the routes on the ground. However, for the benefit of a proper map, we do recommend that you purchase the relevant Ordnance Survey sheet covering your walk. The Ordnance Survey maps are widely available, especially through booksellers and local newsagents.

1 Woodfalls

The Woodfalls Inn

This is a beautiful walk in a tranquil area in the north-west of the Forest only accessible by narrow lanes. Magnificent beech and oak woods sweep down to the Avon valley. We follow woodland paths to discover Hatchet Green, a delightfully friendly village far removed from the bustle of the 21st century, with its central green wide enough for a cricket pitch and thatched white-walled houses. Surprisingly – for the remoteness of the area – the Victorian school has over ninety pupils! From the village we follow part of the Avon Valley Path then leave it to stray over the border into Wiltshire and walk through Woodfalls to return to our starting point, the Woodfalls Inn.

The New Forest

Distance – 3 miles.

OS Explorer OL22 New Forest. GR 198198.

Woodland paths and quiet lanes.

Starting point The Woodfalls Inn.

How to get there From the point where the M27 becomes the A31, take the B3079 towards Fordingbridge. In Brook turn onto the B3078 then take the B3080 towards Downton. The road runs through part of Hale to a junction. Keep to the B3080 as it curves right and the Woodfalls Inn is about 150 yards further on your right. Customers may leave their cars in the pub car park while they are walking.
Public transport: Wilts and Dorset buses to Woodfalls Cross.
☎ 01202 673555 or 01722 336855

THE PUB I can thoroughly recommend the friendly, family-run, award-winning **Woodfalls Inn**, which, in the traditional manner, is open all day to offer food and shelter to the traveller. It is a genuine village hostelry welcoming locals and visitors alike. Originally the inn was a beer and cider house standing on one of the old pilgrimage routes to Salisbury. Today modern features such as a sunny conservatory have been added without harming the old world atmosphere. You can relax in the spacious bar area or the charming snug with its open fireplace and comfortable armchairs. Five real ales are on offer and there is a varied and tempting menu. Among the wide range of dishes you will find Chicken New York – chicken breast wrapped in bacon and cheese – and wild boar sausages, and for a dessert why not try dark chocolate truffle torte or 'Eton mess' – fresh strawberries with meringue and cream. Excellent overnight accommodation is also available and the inn is pet friendly.

The bar is open all day from 11 am to 11 pm. Breakfast is served from 7 am to 9 pm, lunch from 12 noon to 2.30 pm and dinner from 6.30 pm to 10 pm.
☎ *01725 513222; website: www.woodfallsinn.co.uk*

1 Leave the inn by the main entrance and turn left to pass the **Sports and Social Club** on your left. Shortly you enter Hampshire, passing the county sign. At the junction keep straight on over the main road, following the sign for **Woodgreen** along **Hale Road**. Go through the gate by the cattle grid and bear left at the junction signed for **Hale Purlieu** and **Woodgreen** to a crossroads. Keep straight on steeply downhill to pass a track on your right.

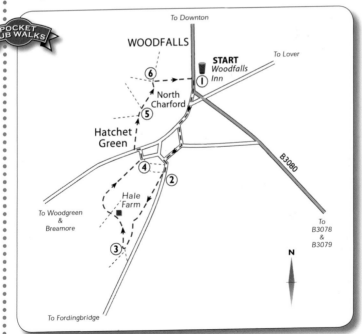

The New Forest

Hatchet Green.

2 Just past a 40 limit sign turn right through the gate immediately on your right by a fingerpost indicating a bridleway. (Ignore the other track on your right leading to a private house.) A woodland path winds for about ¾ mile to a crosspath.

3 Turn right, following the bridleway sign, to take another woodland path shaded by fine beech trees. Keep ahead over a crossing track, still following the bridleway sign, and continue uphill to a gravel road. Cross the road and follow the bridleway sign up to a small gate. Go through and cross the grass ahead to another small gate in front of a barn. From the gate follow the path as it bears a little right past **Hale Farm**. Go through the next gate and follow the attractive bridleway with beech woods on your right and meadows on your left. Continue along the bridleway past a footpath on your right to meet a crossing track. Keep ahead to follow the track towards the houses of **Hatchet Green**. Soon you reach the lanes surrounding a wide green. Don't miss the carving on the green a little to your right. It is believed to be a horse and was carved by a local sculptor to commemorate the millennium.

4 Turn left with the cricket pitch on your right to a T-junction, then turn left again for a few yards to an iron gate on your right. Go through the gate to follow part of the **Avon Valley Path**. Continue past **Hatchet Gate Farm** with a fence on your right. When the fence turns right keep straight ahead downhill and look carefully for a stile leading into woods. Cross the stile, continue over another stile and descend through woodland.

5 Just after a private track leads off your track on the left, the way divides. Leave the **Avon Valley Path** at this point and turn right along a clear path winding along the side of a valley. This soon becomes a wide track. Now for some careful navigation that appears to me to be very odd! Just before the track begins to descend to curve left and run uphill, look for a yellow arrow footpath sign on a post in the valley on your left. Apparently we are intended to leave the track and follow the signs on posts to cross the shallow valley to rejoin the track on the top of the hill! Turn left through a gate and follow an asphalt drive to a crosstrack.

6 Turn right to walk through **Woodfalls** to the B3080 and turn left to the **Woodfalls Inn**.

Places of interest nearby

Breamore House, Anglo-Saxon church and Countryside Museum, to the west of Woodfalls, just off the A338. The house was completed in 1583 by William Dodington, auditor of the Tower Mint. Later the house passed to Sir Edward Hulse and it is still the Hulse family home. Opening times vary.
☎ *01725 512468 or 512233*

2 The Avon Water Meadows & Frankenbury

The Surma Valley Inn

Contrasting scenery and historic interest combine to make this a fascinating circuit. We begin the walk in the Avon valley following a footpath through the lush water meadows west of the river, crossing bridges over willow-bordered streams and rustling reed beds. In spring these wetlands provide breeding areas for lapwings, redshanks and snipe and later in the year they are home to a wealth of other birds including reed buntings, reed warblers and blackcaps. Among the wild flowers fringing the streams and dotting the meadows are kingcups, yellow flag irises, purple loosestrife and the drooping bells of purple and white comfrey. Then, a complete contrast, as we take a woodland path skirting the ramparts of Frankenbury Iron

Distance – 3 miles.

OS Explorer OL22 New Forest. GR 152156.

Water meadows and woodland. NB: The route of this walk runs through a quiet corner of Sandy Balls Estate, now the site of a Holiday Village.

Starting point The Surma Valley Inn, Lower Burgate.

How to get there *The Surma Valley Inn lies beside the A338 Christchurch to Salisbury road in Lower Burgate just north of Fordingbridge. Customers may leave their cars in the pub car park while they are walking.*
Public transport: There is a National Express request bus stop close to the Surma Valley Inn (☎ Traveline: 0870 608 2608).

Age hill fort to a magnificent viewpoint before rejoining our outbound route to return to our starting point, the Tudor Rose Inn near Fordingbridge.

THE PUB The **Surma Valley Inn**, with its gleaming white walls and deep thatch, dates from the sixteenth century. It has been skillfully renovated to preserve its old interior where you will receive a warm and friendly welcome. In the bar area you can relax in comfortable leather seating beside a large inglenook fireplace. The restaurant is very attractive with large French windows opening in good weather to the terrace and gardens. And this is a pub with a difference! If you enjoy a really geat curry chosen from a very varied menu then this is the inn for you. The mouth-watering dishes on offer include Chicken or Lamb Tikka Massala marinated in herbs and spices, barbecued in a tandoor and finished in a mild to medium creamy sauce. Sea Bass Biran, whole sea bass spiced with herbs and spices and fried with

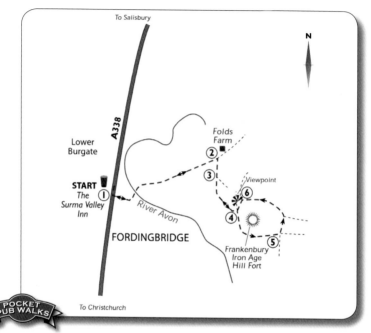

bhuna sauce and Duck Tikka, diced duck marinated in yoghurt with medium spices. Although the menu is predominately Indian there is an English Menu which includes Lemon Sole cooked in white wine and creamy mushroom sauce and Sirloin or Rump steaks grilled or panfried, served with chips, fried onions, fried mushrooms and a salad garnish. There is also an equally extensive Takeaway menu. It is a good plan to book a table as the inn does get very busy. Comfortable overnight accommodation is available.

The inn is open all the week including Bank Holidays. Lunch is served from 12 noon to 2.30 pm and dinner from 5 pm to 11 pm.
☎ *01425 656002 or 01425 652348; website: www.surmavalley.com*

The Avon Water Meadows

1 Cross the road in front of the **Surma Valley Inn** with care and follow the fingerpost indicating the **Avon Valley Path**. The concrete track leads between fields then through a farmyard. Turn left, following the footpath sign, to continue along the Avon Valley Path and cross the suspension bridge over the **Avon**. The river supports over twenty species of fish so you may see herons and kingfishers. The path runs through the water meadows for almost ¾ mile and becomes a track.

2 As you approach the barns of **Folds Farm** the track rises slightly. Look carefully for a track on the right with a post beside it marked with a yellow arrow footpath sign. Turn right and follow the track ahead for about 300 yards with trees on your right and a fenced meadow on your left.

3 Before the track rises and begins to curve left look carefully for a narrow path marked with a yellow arrow footpath sign descending through woodland on your right. Leave the track (you will see a 'Private' sign on a tree beside the track) and turn right through the woods. The path is bordered by fine oak and beech trees. On your left the woods rise steeply. These inaccessible

Crossing the Avon water meadows.

The New Forest

hillsides provide a safe refuge for many animals including deer and badgers. Go through a gate into a meadow and bear left to re-enter woodland, following the path which climbs and curves right to run beside the outer ramparts of **Frankenbury Iron Age hill fort**. It is possible that the leader of the Romano-British, Natan-Leod, camped with his army in this fort around AD 500 before he was defeated by Saxon invaders led by Cerdic on the banks of the Avon at nearby Charford.

4 Cross a stile on your left and walk up to a wide crosspath. Turn right with ramparts on your left. The path curves left round the ramparts through the beech trees then crosses a cleared area to a crosstrack.

5 Turn left to continue to another crosstrack. Turn left again and follow the track uphill, curving left to a gate.

6 Do not go through the gate but climb the knoll on your left for a magnificent view over the **Avon valley**. Descend the knoll and take the footpath on your right, which runs steeply downhill to rejoin our outbound track. Turn right to retrace your steps, turning right at the division then following the track as it curves right. Look for the gate on your left you went through outbound and follow the woodland path to meet the crosstrack. Turn left, then left again to retrace your route along the **Avon Valley Path** to the **Surma Valley Inn**.

Places of interest nearby

Fordingbridge with its magnificent seven-arched bridge over the Avon is an attractive small market town with many excellent shops and an interesting museum charting over 100 years of the area's social and domestic history. It is housed in an old provender mill next to the Information Centre in King's Yard off the High Street.

3 Penn Common & Bramshaw Wood

The Lamb Inn

Richly contrasting scenery is a feature of this walk around the small village of Bramshaw close to the north-eastern border of the Forest. From the pub in Nomansland attractive grass-bordered lanes lead us across part of Penn Common, an undulating area of lush meadows and paddocks, dotted with farms. Patches of heathland are grazed by cattle, sheep and pigs turned out at appropriate times of the year by

The New Forest

the Commoners exercising their ancient rights. Then we enter a different world as we return through some of the Forest's most beautiful woods where massive oak and beech trees provide a haven for wildlife.

THE PUB Many country pubs have changed their character in the last few years but not the **Lamb Inn**! This is a genuine traditional Forest pub with a warm welcome and a delightfully friendly atmosphere. If you wonder how the village received its intriguing name, a document on one of the walls will provide

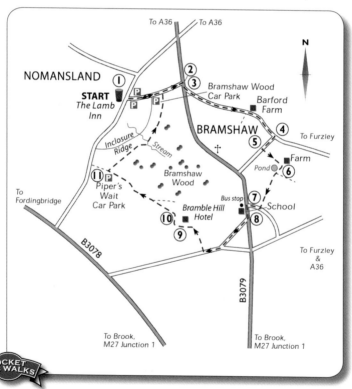

Distance – 4 miles.

OS Explorer OL22 New Forest. GR 254173.

Commons and woodland.

Starting point The Lamb Inn, Nomansland.

How to get there The best approach is via the A36. Turn for Nomansland in Plaitford. Continue along the minor road for about 2½ miles and the Lamb Inn is on your right. Or approach via the B3078 Fordingbridge road and continue north for about 2 miles to the pub on your left. Park in one of the car parks either side of the lane opposite the pub.
Public transport: As the walk is circular you can start and finish in Bramshaw by catching a Wilts and Dorset bus (☎ 01202 673555 or 01722 336855). There is a request stop opposite the school, point 7 on the walk.

you with clues. Other walls are decorated with old photographs of the village and its residents. A varied menu includes crispy Yorkshire puddings filled with sausage and onions and jacket potatoes with a choice of thirteen different fillings. More substantial meals might be steak and ale pie and roasted shoulder of lamb. Ringwood and Strongs of Romsey provide local ales and there is an extensive wine list. Well-behaved dogs on leads are welcome.

Opening times on Monday to Thursday are 11 am to 3 pm and 6 pm to 11 pm; Friday and Saturday 11 am to 11 pm; Sunday 12 noon to 10.30 pm. Food is served from 12 noon to 2.30 pm and 6.30 pm to 9.30 pm (it is wise to book at weekends).
☎ 01794 390246

The New Forest

[1] With your back to the pub head east along the lane away from the village. Follow the lane past several car parks, including **Bramshaw Wood car park** on your right, for about ¾ mile to meet the B3079 road.

[2] Cross the road and turn right to follow a pleasant footpath through the trees to the left of the road to the turning for **Newbridge**.

[3] Turn left to follow the Newbridge lane across **Penn Common**. Continue for about a mile past **Barford Farm** to a lane on the right signed to **Bramshaw** and **Fritham**.

[4] Bear right along the lane for about ¼ mile to a footpath sign on the left by a white-railed footbridge.

[5] Turn left over the bridge and take the track ahead leading to a brick-built farm. Just before the farm, pass a pond on your right and turn almost immediately right (there is a yellow arrow footpath sign on the wooden post supporting electric cables). Cross the grass, bearing slightly left for a few yards, and look carefully for a stile leading into the wood on your right.

[6] Cross the stile and walk straight ahead through the wood to go over another stile into a meadow. Walk across the meadow with a fence on your left. Follow the line of the fence to cross another stile and continue to a track. Turn right and walk down to the B3079 in **Bramshaw village**.

[7] The school is almost directly opposite (your starting point if you are using the bus). Turn left through the village for about 100 yards to an unsigned lane on your right.

[8] Turn right and follow the lane to a road. Bear right for about

A tree-shaded pond on Penn Common.

100 yards then turn right again up the drive leading to **Bramble Hill Hotel**. Shortly you will see the hotel on the hillside on your right.

9 As the drive passes the side of the hotel look carefully for a narrow gravel track on your left and a footpath sign. Turn left and follow the track as it curves right uphill to meet the drive opposite the clock tower on the former stables.

10 Turn left to go through a gate and follow the path into **Bramshaw Wood**. After a few yards the path divides and you can choose

either the footpath (a footprint) or the bridleway (a horseshoe). Take the left hand path – the bridleway – and enjoy strolling straight ahead through these lovely woods. Keep to the main track, ignoring all side paths, for about ¾ mile heading north-west. The path rises to open heathland. Bear right for a few yards then resume heading north-west along a good path over the heath. On your right there is a wonderful view.

11 The path brings you to **Piper's Wait car park**. Turn right with your back to the car park and follow the partly gravelled path into the wood. After about 100 yards you meet a crosstrack. Turn left and follow the path downhill heading north-east. The path may be indistinct at times but keep ahead and shortly you will see the embankment marking the edge of **Bramshaw Inclosure** on your left. The path follows the line of the embankment. As you come to the foot of the valley the path appears to cease! Turn right to cross a stream in a gully then continue heading north-east along the main track, which rises to bring you to **Bramshaw Wood car park** and the lane you followed to begin the walk. Turn left to return to the **Lamb Inn**.

Places of interest nearby

The **Bramble Hill Hotel** welcomes walkers. It is an interesting building, mostly Victorian in character but it is built around the core of an old Forest lodge and retains features dating back to medieval times. There is a comfortable bar for drinks and meals, which include cream teas.
☎ *02380 813165*

4 **FRITHAM**

The Royal Oak

A **track that disappears into woodland** leads you to Fritham, a remote village surrounded by some of the wildest and most interesting areas of the Forest. Today the village, set among wide greens, presents an idyllic scene but during the 19th century it was at the centre of a thriving industry when the Schultze gunpowder works was established close by at Eyeworth. The stream in the valley was dammed to provide water for cooling purposes and now Eyeworth Pond is a beautiful lake, carpeted with white waterlilies. We take meadow paths round the village, then head north over Longcross Plain, a glorious sight in late summer when the heather is in bloom. We follow an embanked track made to support the waggons leaving the Schultze works, then follow the shoreline of Eyeworth Pond before returning to our starting point in Fritham village.

THE PUB

The **Royal Oak Inn** is just the kind of pub you would expect to find in woodland over nine hundred years old! Welcoming and homely, it is deep-thatched with an enormous open fireplace where hams once hung to smoke. The two small bar areas are beautifully cared for and the oak fittings were carved by local craftsmen. From a little bay window you can look out over green New Forest lawns and grazing ponies. Ringwood real ales are served from the cask and delicious soups, ploughman's, salads and pies are available at lunchtimes. The pub is dog and walker friendly.

Opening times are from 11 am to 3 pm and 6 pm to 11 pm on weekdays. On Saturday the pub is open all day from 11 am to 11 pm and on Sunday from 12 noon to 10.30 pm. Lunches only are supplied in summer. In winter meals are available on Monday or Tuesday evenings but you will need to book beforehand.
☎ *02380 812606*

Distance – 4 miles.

OS Explorer OL22 New Forest. GR 231140.

Interesting village and landscape.

Starting point Fritham car park, close to the Royal Oak.

How to get there *From the Cadnam roundabout follow the B3079, signed to Brook and Bramshaw. Just past the Bell Inn in Brook take the B3078 for Fordingbridge and turn left for Fritham. Take the second turning on the right to drive through the village past the Royal Oak to the car park on your left. Public transport: There is an infrequent bus service to Fritham run by Wilts and Dorset buses (☎ 01202 673555 or 01722 336855). Also Solent Blue Line (☎ 02380 618233).*

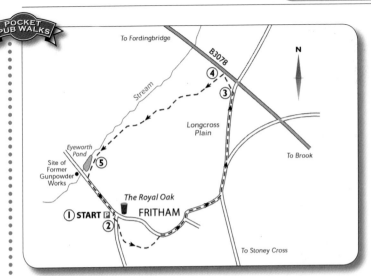

To Fordingbridge

B3078

N

④

③

Stream

Longcross Plain

Eyeworth Pond

Site of Former Gunpowder Works

⑤

To Brook

The Royal Oak

① START 🅿 FRITHAM

②

To Stoney Cross

To Stoney Cross

1 From the car park in **Fritham** cross the grass in the direction of the **Royal Oak**. Just before the inn, turn right along a narrow lane, leaving a sign marked 'Forestry Commision, No Through Road' on your right. Houses face the lane on your left (the first house is **Valletta Cottage**). Shortly you pass the little brick-built **Free Church Chapel** built in 1904. Magnificent oak trees with their skirts of protective holly shade the green lawns on your right.

2 Just past the last house, turn left, following the footpath sign down a grass and gravel track. When the track curves right, keep ahead through a gate and follow a grassy path to go through another gate. Walk up the meadow, keeping a hedge close on your right. Cross a stile on your right and follow a narrow path that leads over another stile and curves left. Continue with a hedge on your left to go through a gate and follow the fenced path to go through a small iron gate. Cross the paddock ahead where another iron gate opens to a lane. Turn right and follow the lane for just over ½ mile, bearing left at the junction to meet the road heading north over **Longcross Plain** towards the B3078.

The New Forest

3 Turn left to walk over the heath beside the road. Just before you come to the B3078, turn left to cut the corner and meet the road by a Forestry Commission barrier.

4 Turn left to follow the good embanked track for almost 2 miles, heading south-west to enter woodland and descend into the **Eyeworth valley**. Look for a circle of wooden palings on your right surrounding **Irons Well**. This chalybeate spring was considered beneficial for sore eyes. Pass a Forestry Commission barrier to leave the woods and enjoy a delightful walk along the shore of **Eyeworth Pond**. Now a haven for wildlife, it is hard to imagine a gunpowder factory on this site! But until 1910 when the last of the original three leases expired a whole factory complex was located here with huts for the workmen.

5 Follow the track beside the pond to a lane and turn left uphill to **Fritham village**. The car park is on your right and the **Royal Oak** straight ahead.

A description of life in Fritham during the early years of the 20th century can be found in *Fritham, an Ancient New Forest Village* obtainable from Margaret Holgate at Valletta Cottage, Fritham (see point 1 of the walk) or Landford Post Office.

Eyeworth Pond

5 Minstead

The Trusty Servant Inn

Closeness to nature is the charm of the Forest and I feel it applies particularly to Minstead, a small village set among lush meadows, almost completely surrounded by woodland. The central green, grazed by ponies, is overlooked by an ancient church, while a scattering of outlying settlements ramble around a network of narrow lanes. From the village we take a footpath through the meadows and follow a quiet lane to discover Furzey Gardens. The walk continues downhill through beautiful oak and beech woods then follows the road to Newtown – a misleading name for this small hamlet! A pleasant path leads us through the coppiced hazels, oaks and beeches of Manor Wood, before passing Minstead church to return to the road and our starting point close to the Trusty Servant Inn.

The New Forest

Distance – 4½ miles.

OS Explorer OL22 New Forest. GR 282110.

Fascinating village and Furzey Gardens.

Starting point The parking area close to the Trusty Servant Inn.

How to get there *From Lyndhurst take the A337 Romsey road and after about 1½ miles turn left following the directions for Minstead, turning right for the village centre when you see the village sign. The parking area is on your right beside the road opposite the village green. If this is full, drive up the lane to the church (the pub is on your right) and park under the trees beside the churchyard. Return down the lane to begin the walk.*
Public transport: Wilts and Dorset buses (☎ 01202 673555 or 01722 336855. Solent Blue Line (☎ 02380 618233).

THE PUB The friendly **Trusty Servant Inn** facing the village green will soon become a favourite with all the family. Locals and visitors alike enjoy its happy village pub atmosphere. There can be few better ways to pass a summer evening than to sit outside in the large garden with a drink and share the festivities – still an important part to life in Minstead. These include Morris dancing and celebrations at Whitsun and Easter when the Forest Mummers' plays are revived. The inn sign depicts 'the trusty servant' who turns out to be a pig with a padlocked snout to illustrate discretion and stag's feet to indicate speed in running errands. Real ales include Wadworth 6X and there is a wide range of wines. The extensive menu includes a splendid choice of fresh seafood, for example blue marlin, swordfish and red snapper. Dogs on leads are welcome. The inn also offers overnight accommodation.

Minstead Walk 5

The inn is open six days a week from 11 am to 11 pm and on Sundays from 12 noon to 10.30 pm. Meals are served from 12 noon to 2 pm and from 7 pm to 9 pm.
☎ *02380 812137*

1 Turn right from the parking area to walk up the road, passing the village green and the lane to the church on your left. The **Trusty Servant Inn** is on the corner. Follow the road past a lane on the right. Shortly after, you pass a lane on the left and a few yards further on take the footpath running parallel with the road on your right. When it rejoins the road continue a little further and look for a stile by a footpath sign on the left.

2 Cross the stile and walk down the field ahead with a hedge on your right. Cross a stile and a small footbridge and continue up the field to cross a stile to a lane.

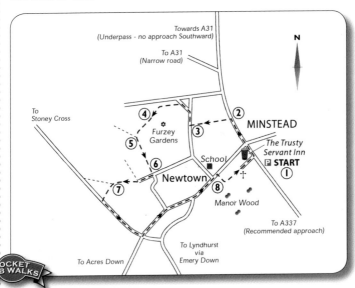

The New Forest

Minstead churchyard, with Sir Arthur Conan Doyle's grave in the foreground.

3 Turn right up the lane to a T-junction. Turn left to walk up the lane and take the track on the left leading to the entrance to **Furzey Gardens**.

4 After a visit to the gardens return to the track and turn left, with the gardens on your left, to enter woodland. Shortly the track divides. Take the right hand track. After going through a gate the track bears slightly left downhill to lead you over a small footbridge. Keep ahead past another gate to a track and turn left. Continue downhill to follow a stepped boardwalk and cross a bridge. The track now runs uphill to a fence. Bear left to a stile.

5 Cross the stile and follow the narrow path downhill to go over a bridge and walk uphill to a further stile.

6 Cross the stile and turn immediately right, following the bridleway sign. The asphalt gives way to gravel and after about 50 yards

the track divides. Keep ahead (left hand track) uphill for about ¼ mile when the track divides again.

7 Take the left hand track, which curves uphill past a track on the left to meet the road between **Stoney Cross** and **Emery Down**. Turn left to walk beside the road to a crossroads. Bear left for about ½ mile to **Newtown**. The road descends to a bridge and ford opposite the school.

8 Cross the bridge and turn almost immediately right over a gravelled area then turn left through a gate, following the footpath sign into **Manor Wood**. The coppiced trees are a reminder that Minstead was once an important centre for the production of charcoal. The path continues beside the church, one of the most fascinating in the Forest. It is built of traditional Forest materials – wattle filled with rubble and daub. Among much of interest is a rare three-decker pulpit. In the southern edge of the churchyard is the grave of Sir Arthur Conan Doyle who lived in the Forest at Bignell Wood. Walk down the lane past the war memorial and the stocks to return to your car.

Places of interest nearby

Do enjoy a visit to **Furzey Gardens** where magnificent azaleas and rhododendrons flourish on the acid soil. Children love coming here as there is a woodland area with tree houses for them to scramble about in. Close to the entrance of this true Forest garden you can visit a 400-year-old cottage. It has only two tiny bedrooms but it once housed a family with fourteen children! Beside the cottage a large gallery displays a variety of local arts and crafts. The gardens are open throughout the year from 10 am to 5 pm. Light refreshments are available.
☎ *02380 812464; website: www.furzey-gardens.org*

6 Lyndhurst

The Mailman's Arms

The great historian of the Forest, John Wise, writing in 1883, stated that the people of Lyndhurst possessed 'a wider park and nobler trees than even Royalty'. He could say the same today. Only a short walk away from Lyndhurst's bustling High Street the Forest's varied scenery of oak and beech woods, open heath and fine views is waiting for you to enjoy. This walk leads you along the high ground east of Lyndhurst known as The Ridge, giving wide views north over heathland and south to the great woods of Matley and Denny. Then we take woodland paths through old inclosures, home to many wild creatures including deer and badgers, before returning to Lyndhurst, crossing The Ridge along a different path.

Distance – 3½ miles.

OS Explorer OL22 New Forest. GR 303082.

Capital of the Forest and fine views.

Starting point Bolton's Bench car park, just east of Lyndhurst.

How to get there *Leave Lyndhurst along the A35 towards Southampton and turn right along the B3056, the Beaulieu road. Turn immediately left into Bolton's Bench car park.*
Public transport: Wilts and Dorset bus service to Lyndhurst
☎ *01202 673555 or 01722 336855). There is a stop close to Bolton's Bench car park, which is only a few minutes walk from the village centre.*

THE PUB

Well known for its beautiful floral displays and delightful secluded garden, the **Mailman's Arms** is a traditional friendly family pub. The spacious bar area is maintained to a very high standard with comfortable leather seating. Real ales are Greene King IPA and Abbot Ale and Morland Old Speckled Hen. The comprehensive menu includes a wide range of sandwiches, baguettes and snacks as well as full meals including tasty pies, mixed grills and our special favourite – poached salmon on a bed of couscous with tarragon sauce. Excellent overnight accommodation is also available.

Opening times are 11 am to 11 pm on weekdays and 12 noon to 10.30 pm on Sundays. During the week food is served from 12 noon to 3 pm and 6.30 pm to 10 pm; on Saturdays from 12 noon to 10 pm; on Sundays from 12 noon to 9.30 pm.
☎ *02380 284196; website: info@mailmans-arms.co.uk*

The New Forest

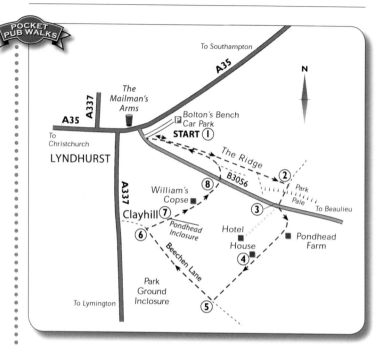

POCKET PUB WALKS

To Southampton

A35

N

The Mailman's Arms

A337

A35

Bolton's Bench Car Park
START ①

To Christchurch

LYNDHURST

The Ridge

B3056

②

Park Pale

To Beaulieu

A337

William's Copse ■

⑧

Clayhill ⑦

Pondhead Inclosure

③

⑥

Beechen Lane

Hotel

House

■ Pondhead Farm

④

Park Ground Inclosure

To Lymington

⑤

1 From the car park bear left up the lane past the war memorial. The cone-shaped hill on your right topped by a yew tree is **Bolton's Bench**, named after Lord Bolton who was Lord Warden of the Forest in 1688. Continue uphill, passing the drive to the cemetery on your left. Go past a Forestry Commission barrier and continue uphill along the gravel track. As you gain height look back for a beautiful view over the trees to **Lyndhurst**. The large white building on the hill is **Northerwood House**, which was once visited by George IV who gave it the name of 'Mount Royal'. Continue along the ridge-top gravel path as it runs parallel to the Beaulieu road, for about ¾ mile past a path on the right. The path dips a little downhill and at the foot you meet a narrow crosspath. It runs to the right of a black and white house by the roadside.

2 Turn right to walk down the heath towards the road. The path cuts through **Park Pale**, a medieval earth embankment that once enclosed Lyndhurst Old Park, a deer park about two hundred acres in extent. When Charles II enclosed New Park near Brockenhurst the old park was no longer needed. On reaching the road, on your right you will see a large sign for **Le Poussin restaurant** and a sign for **Pondhead Farm**.

3 Cross the road and turn left, following the sign for the farm along a lane with **Pondhead Farm** on your left. Keep ahead over open grassland. Just after you pass a house on your right the gravel ceases and the path becomes indistinct and can be muddy after heavy rain.

4 Bear a few steps to your left then resume your former heading through the bracken, keeping a fence about 30 yards away on your right, leading through the oak and beech woods of **Park Hill Inclosure**. With the fence now about 50 yards away on your right, cross a small wooden bridge. Continue ahead. After about ½ mile you come to a gravel crossing track, **Beechen Lane**.

On The Ridge, near Lyndhurst.

The New Forest

5 Turn right to follow **Beechen Lane**, which runs between **Park Ground Inclosure** and **Pondhead Inclosure** for about ¾ mile.

6 Go through a gate out of the woods at **Clayhill** and turn immediately right to go through another gate to follow a track through **Pondhead Inclosure**. This inclosure has very high fences to prevent deer and stock from entering, and in late spring it is carpeted with bluebells.

7 At the division take the left hand path. After about 100 yards look carefully to the left of the path where a plaque on a wooden post marks **William's Copse**. In 1979 a hundred sessile oaks were planted here to commemorate the 900th anniversary of the creation of the New Forest by William the Conqueror. Cross a bridge, go through two gates to leave the inclosure.

8 Keep ahead to cross the Beaulieu road and walk up the heath to **The Ridge**. Before you reach the gravel track you come to a wide green crossing path. Turn left to follow this, with the gravel path running parallel on your right to a trig point and a seat. From the seat there is a beautiful view over **Pondhead Inclosure**. Continue along **The Ridge** to rejoin the gravel track and return to **Bolton's Bench car park**. To visit the **Mailman's Arms** turn left at the A35 and the pub is on your right.

Places of interest nearby

No holiday in the Forest is complete without a visit to the excellent **New Forest Museum and Visitor Centre** adjoining Lyndhurst central car park. It gives a richly rewarding insight into all aspects of Forest life.
☎ 02380 283444

7 Ashurst – Around Woodlands

The New Forest Hotel

The name **Woodlands** recalls its ancient origin. This small area north of Ashurst, spreading south from the busy A336 to the New Forest boundary, was originally densely wooded, part of a primeval forest possibly ten thousand years old. Today the forest has been replaced by hedged meadows dotted with coppiced woodland and farms but it is still rich in rare lichens. It is threaded by tiny streams and criss-crossed by surprisingly remote footpaths and lanes. As you follow the route of this walk I think you will agree that this quiet countryside is well worth exploring.

The New Forest

THE PUB The New Forest became popular in Victorian times with the coming of the railway and the **New Forest Hotel**, built in 1881, stood close to Ashurst station to welcome visitors. Among many distinguished guests was the Queen herself. The fame of this friendly Forest pub has spread to the QE2 and I was told that a party of Americans arrived one day wishing to buy one of the bathrooms, which they were told retained its Victorian fittings! Today the old building remains but has been brought up to date with a splendid conservatory and a marquee in summer. While parents relax over a drink in the garden, which overlooks the open Forest, children can enjoy themselves in a fully equipped playground. Dogs should be kept on leads. Fuller's

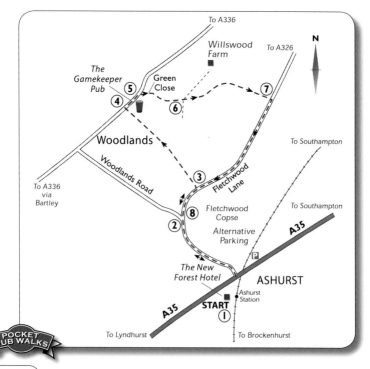

Distance – 3½ miles.

OS Explorer OL22 New Forest. GR 333102.

Interesting area on the north-east border of the Forest.

Starting point The New Forest Hotel car park.

How to get there *The New Forest Hotel is close to the station in Ashurst beside the A35 just west of the village. Its car park is available to customers while they walk. Alternatively, you could park in the Ashurst car park near the entrance to Ashurst Hospital which at present is free.*
Public transport: Wilts and Dorset buses run regular services to Ashurst (☎ 01202 673555 or 01722 336855). Or you can arrive by train (for times and fares ☎ 08457 484950).

real ales are available and a wide range of wines. The extensive menu includes irresistible bar snacks and seafood dishes. The hotel offers overnight accommodation and is perfectly placed for an enjoyable family holiday.

In summer the pub is open from 11 am to 11 pm on Monday to Saturday. In winter the hours are from 11 am to 2.30 pm and from 6 pm to 11 pm. On Sunday normal pub hours apply. Food is served every day from 12 noon to 2 pm and from 6 pm to 9.30 pm.
☎ 02380 292721; website: www.newforestashurst.co.uk

1 Starting from the hotel's car park entrance, turn right beside the A35. After a few yards turn left to cross the road and follow the lane opposite, signed for **Woodlands**. The lane swings left past **Peterscroft Avenue** on the right. Continue along this pleasant

The New Forest

road for just over ½ mile to the turning for **Fletchwood Lane** on your right.

A New Forest glade, near Ashurst.

2 Turn right along **Fletchwood Lane**. **Fletchwood Copse** is on your right and, judging by its name, in the days when the longbow played its part in winning the battles of Agincourt and Crécy, this now privately owned wood must have been important as a source of arrows. Continue along the lane for about ¼ mile to a gravel track on your left.

3 Turn left to walk between houses on your left and a hedge on your right. Go through a gate and keep ahead along an attractive field footpath for about ¾ mile. This leads you through a gate to the road in **Woodlands village**.

4 Bear right past the **Gamekeeper pub** (five real ales and excellent food) and follow the road for about ¼ mile to **Green Close** on your right.

5 Turn right to walk through the Close and follow the footpath sign a little to your left along a gravel track, which soon becomes a path. Cross a stile by a gate and follow the path to cross another stile. Continue along the narrow path ahead with a fence on your right.

6 Navigate carefully at this point as when we came this way the footpath sign was broken. When the fence on your right ceases, leave the main track which leads to **Willswood Farm**, cross a track running down through fields on your right and keep ahead beside a field with a hedge on your left (we saw the remains of the footpath sign indicating the route buried in the hedge). At the end of the field, cross a stile and a small bridge to enter woodland. Follow this lovely path as it winds its way beside a stream for almost a mile to meet **Fletchwood Lane**.

7 Turn right along the road which soon becomes a gravel track past **Great Fletchwood Farm** and **Martins Croft** to return to **Woodlands Road**.

8 Turn left to retrace your steps along **Woodlands Road** to the A35. Turn right to cross the road to the car park at the **New Forest Hotel**.

Places of interest nearby

Longdown Activity Farm, off the A35 south-east of Ashurst. A wonderful day out, especially for children, who can bottle-feed goat kids and calves and enjoy tractor and trailer rides. Gift shop and tea rooms. Open daily from mid February to the end of October, 10 am to 5 pm; also weekends in November and December plus a few days before Christmas.
☎ 02380 293326; website: www.longdownfarm.co.uk

New Forest Otter, Owl and Wildlife Park, also at Longdown. A most enjoyable place as you can experience close encounters with many fascinating animals and birds. Open daily from February to December, 10 am to 6 pm; weekdays only in January.
☎ 02380 292408; website: www.ottersandowls.co.uk

The Drift Inn

The **B3056 road from Lyndhurst** runs over the heath south-east to Beaulieu. At one point the road crosses the main Southampton to Bournemouth railway and here, in the heart of the Forest, you will find Beaulieu Road halt – just a pub, a hotel and a handful of cottages. It is surrounded by wonderful walking country and this short ramble is one of my favourites. We cross heathland with raised causeways over wetlands rich in wild flowers and walk through splendid oak and beech woods where there is every possibility you will see deer.

THE PUB The **Drift Inn** is a traditional Forest hostelry that aims to make all its visitors feel at home. Long, low and rambling, it is an ideal family pub with plenty of room for everyone. There is a spacious bar area and the restaurant can seat up to ninety people.

Real ales are Ringwood Old Thumper and Best, Courage Directors and Fuller's London Pride and there is an extensive wine list. The varied menu includes something for everyone to enjoy, with dishes such as local pork tenderloin, spit roasts and wild mushrooms. The garden overlooks the Forest and there is a play area for children. The New Forest Pony Sales, always an exciting event, take place nearby on the first Thursday of every month.

The pub is open on weekdays from 11 am to 3 pm and from 6 pm to 11 pm; on Saturday and Sunday it is open all day from 11 am to 11 pm. Food is served on weekdays from 12 noon to 3 pm and from 6 pm to 9 pm. At weekends hot food is served during the above times and cold food is available from 3 pm to 5 pm. ☎ 02380 292342; website: www.driftinn.co.uk

1 With your back to the road, walk past the Forestry Commission barrier on your left and follow the path ahead over the heath. In

Distance – 4 miles.

OS Explorer OL22 New Forest. GR 348064.

Heathland and paths in ancient woods.

Starting point Shatterford car park, beside the Lyndhurst to Beaulieu road, close to Beaulieu Road station and the pub.

How to get there Shatterford car park is about 3 miles south-east of Lyndhurst. Approaching from Lyndhurst along the B3056, turn right for the car park just before the railway bridge.
Public transport: You can arrive by train using the main Southampton to Bournemouth service (for train times ☎ 08457 484950).

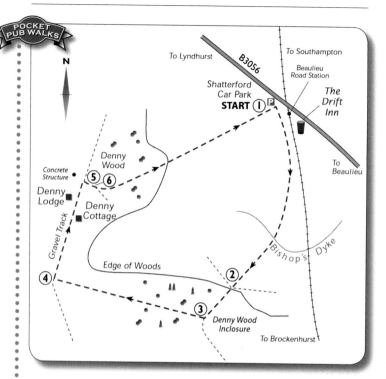

late summer when the heather is in bloom this is a wonderful sight. Keep ahead towards a line of woodland on the horizon. The path is raised above marshy areas scented with bog myrtle. The path cuts through the long line of an earth embankment. This is part of the boundary of **Bishop's Dyke** enclosing a marshy expanse about a mile in length and half a mile wide, which until quite recently belonged to the Bishop of Winchester. In 1284 the Bishop persuaded Edward I to enclose the land but no one knows why!

2 As you approach the woods through a fringe of silver birches you come to a fine oak tree at the junction of several paths. Keep straight ahead over a crossing track and go through a gate into

Denny Wood Inclosure. A grassy path leads ahead and then curves round to the right.

3 The main path then curves left. Do not follow it but keep straight ahead, passing the main path on your left. Keep straight ahead through this remote and beautiful woodland for about a mile until you meet a gravel track.

4 Turn right and follow the gravel track through a gate. The track leads past **Denny Cottage** on your right and **Denny Lodge** on your left and becomes asphalt. Continue for about 30 yards and look left for a large concrete structure.

5 Opposite the structure turn right along a faint path through the trees. After about 100 yards you will see two clear paths ahead.

6 Follow the left hand path which curves left, maintaining your height to lead you through the fine oak and beech woods of **Denny**. You emerge from the wood onto the open heath again and over the heath you will see **Shatterford car park** and the cottages at **Beaulieu Road station** on the horizon. Follow the path back to your car. Cross the railway bridge to visit the pub.

Places of interest nearby

Beaulieu Abbey, Palace House and Motor Museum. Open May to September 10 am to 6 pm; October to April 10 am to 5 pm.
☎ 01590 612123; website: www.beaulieu.co.uk

A delightful day can be spent at **Bucklers Hard**, south-east of Beaulieu, a perfectly preserved 18th century village with a fascinating museum and cottages illustrating Forest life at that time. Ships for Nelson's navy were built here and you can see the remains of the slipways.
☎ 01590 616203; website: www.bucklershard.co.uk

The Snakecatcher

Brockenhurst is a large village surrounded by beautiful woods and heaths interlaced with streams. North of the village the upper reaches of the Lymington river runs through dense woods and to the west a smaller stream, Ober Water, flows to join it near New Park, Charles II's favourite hunting lodge. This walk follows a streamside footpath from the village centre to follow the course of the Lymington river. Then we take woodland paths beside the Ober Water stream before crossing a footbridge to the heath and following a track around North Weirs with glorious views over White Moor to the woods of Hincheslea.

Distance – 5 miles.

OS Explorer OL22 New Forest. GR 299023.

Rivers and streams.

Starting point Brockenhurst central car park off Brookley Road.

How to get there *Brockenhurst lies beside the A337 Lyndhurst to Lymington road. Approaching from Lyndhurst, turn off the A337 along the B3055 following the sign for Sway to meet Brookley Road at the crossroads in the village centre. Turn right down Brookley Road, then shortly turn right again opposite the post office into the pay-and-display car park. If you plan a longer stay than four hours drive to the far end of the car park where you can park for up to eight hours.*
Public transport: Wilts and Dorset buses (☎ 01202 673555 or 01722 336855). Train: South West Train service (☎ 08457 484950).

THE PUB

If you want to visit a genuine warm-hearted New Forest pub where you will be welcomed by the locals as well as the bar staff then the **Snakecatcher**, in Lyndhurst Road near the station, is for you! It was featured on TV when a programme was made about a famous Forest snakecatcher, Harry Mills. He was known as 'Brusher Mills' as his other occupations included sweeping Lyndhurst cricket pitch. He lived in a hut in the Forest and was a regular at the Railway Inn, now called the Snakecatcher in his memory. Find out all about this fascinating character from the detailed accounts and photographs on the walls.

An excellent menu offers a comprehensive range of snacks including jacket potatoes with delicious fillings as well as full meals such as beef and ale pie and home-cooked ham with

The New Forest

eggs and bourbon sauce. Real ales are Brakspear, Wychwood Hobgoblin and John Smith's. Dogs are welcome and there is a well-shaded garden.

The pub is open every day except Sunday from 11 am to 11 pm. On Sunday the pub opens at 12 noon. Food is served all day.
☎ *01590 622348*

1 Turn right from the car park entrance and walk down **Brookley Road** to cross the watersplash. Turn right and follow the white railings by the stream. When these end look for some small bridges leading over the stream to the houses. Look carefully just by the second bridge and you will see a small wooden gate opening to a streamside footpath.

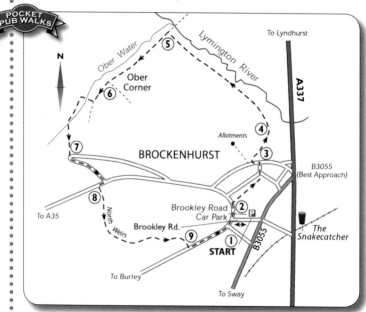

Ober Water stream.

2 Turn left through the gate and follow the path to a lane by a watersplash. Turn left and walk up to a road near a phone box.

3 Bear left beside the road for a few yards to a track on the right leading to allotments. Do not follow the track to the allotments but turn right along a path beside a little stream, keeping the stream on your right. Ahead you will see the long line of trees that border the **Lymington river**. Opposite a bridge on your right the path bears a little left and heads for the line of woodland.

4 When you reach the woods, turn left and follow the path close to the trees on your right. The river winds through the woods a short distance away. At one point the path is overgrown for about 30 yards. Circle round it over the grass then resume your former heading close to the edge of the woods. Continue until you meet a gravel track.

5 Turn left beside the track. The **Ober Water** stream flows through the woods on your right. Keep ahead to go past a Forestry Commission barrier to a road at **Ober Corner**.

The New Forest

6 Keep straight on along the road and after about ¼ mile turn right along the track to **Aldridge Hill** camp site and cross the bridge over **Ober Water**. Turn left to follow the streamside through beautiful woodland, soon coming to a wider path. After about ¼ mile you will see another footbridge. Turn left to cross the bridge and keep straight ahead along a pleasant path fringed with pines to a road.

7 Bear a little right then follow the road with trees on your left to walk past a car park to meet the road that runs west from Brockenhurst to join the A35.

8 Over the road a few yards to your right you will see a gravel track. Cross the road and follow this track with the houses of **North Weirs** on your left and the open heathland of **White Moor** on your right. The track curves left round **North Weirs** to meet the Brockenhurst to Burley road.

9 Turn left and follow the tracks and footpaths to the left of the road to the watersplash at the foot of **Brookley Road**. Turn right and walk up the road and turn left to return to your car. Or continue up the road to the **Snakecatcher pub**.

The Queen's Head

Burley **is an attractive village** in the south-west of the Forest, its busy main street lined with craft and souvenir shops, a magnet for all who visit the area. But it is still very much a walkers' village surrounded by remote heathland valleys and old oak woods. This walk takes you south of the village where the heathland has a character all its own. The path dips and rises over shallow valleys and miniature hills presenting unexpected glimpses of a hidden Forest lawn, a half-concealed stream or a lonely wood. We walk downhill to follow the track of the former railway, which once ran west across the Forest to Poole, before returning over the heath to Burley.

The New Forest

The friendly **Queen's Head** describes itself as 'a country pub with country ways'. The building dates back to 1645 and retains many old world features with delightful nooks, alcoves and crannies where you can tuck yourself away to enjoy a meal and drink. During the 18th and early 19th centuries it was a favourite smugglers' haunt and most of the paths leading from the pub into the Forest are smugglers' tracks. Records tell of a secret tunnel leading from the pub to Burley Manor and a smugglers' cellar with pistols, bottles and old coins was discovered under one of the bars. No doubt they enjoyed the pub's excellent food as much as we do today! The menu is extensive and varied and can include traditional baked lasagne and beef and ale pie and among the desserts a chocolate mousse cake served with chocolate sauce and a jug of fresh double cream. Real ales are Greene King IPA and Abbot Ale and a rotating guest chosen from Ringwood Best/Fortyniner and Tisbury Ale Fresco.

Distance – 3 miles.

OS Explorer OL22 New Forest. GR 214029.

Village lanes and heathland.

Starting point Burley Cricket car park, close to Burley village.

How to get there Turn for Burley off the A35. Drive past the Burley village sign on the left and shortly after turn right into Burley Cricket car park.

Public transport: Wilts and Dorset bus service to Burley village (☎ 01202 673555 or 01722 336855). Alight at the stop by the Queen's Head pub and walk up the hill opposite the front of the pub. Turn right opposite the school to begin the walk at point 2.

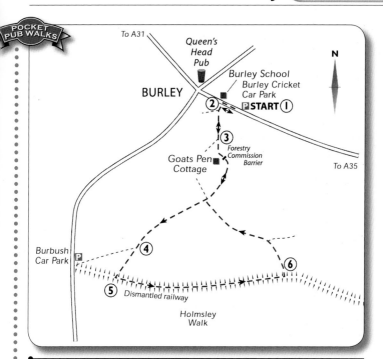

*Opening times are from 11 am to 11 pm seven days a week.
Food is served on Monday to Saturday from 12 noon to 10 pm
and on Sunday from 11 am to 9.30 pm.*
☎ *01425 403423*

1 Return to the car park entrance, cross the road and turn right in
the direction of Burley. Walk beside the road for about 30 yards
to a wide gravelled bus turning area on your left opposite the
school. There is a sign for **Moorhill House Hotel** on the corner.

2 Turn left over the turning area to follow a gravelled track to a
division. Turn left, following the sign for **Moorhill House Hotel**.

The New Forest

The track becomes an asphalt lane. Follow the lane downhill to a sign on the left indicating the track to **Goats Pen Cottage**.

3 Turn left to follow the track to the cottage. Pass the side of the cottage on your right. Bear right to the front of the cottage and facing it you will see a wooden Forestry Commission barrier. Turn left past the barrier and keep ahead over the grass for a few yards. Continue along the main path (left hand path) at the division. The path climbs onto the heath, curving a little right, and soon becomes a wide gravel track, very easy to follow, rising and dipping over the heath. After about ¾ mile the track dips into a valley beneath power lines and divides.

4 Keep straight ahead (left hand path) to climb the opposite hill. The track now descends to meet the track of the dismantled railway line.

Goats Pen Plain.

5 Turn left to follow this pleasant way, bordered at first with wild roses and brambles and shaded by young oak trees. These give way to open heathland with wide views to the right over **Holmsley Walk**. Follow the disused track for about a mile until you come to a gravel track on the left leading down to a causeway over a marshy area.

6 Turn left into the valley and continue over the causeway. On either side thickets of bog myrtle (known in the Forest as gold withey) flourish in these wetlands, filling the air with their pungent scent. Keep to the same path as it bears a little left uphill onto the open heath. When you come to a crossing track bear left still uphill. At the top of the hill the path divides. Take the right hand path to walk the few yards to meet the track you followed outbound from **Goats Pen Cottage** where you turn right to retrace your steps, leaving **Goats Pen Cottage** on your left. Bear right to the road. Turn right up the lane, then right again to the road opposite **Burley school**. Turn left downhill to visit the **Queen's Head pub** or right to return to your car.

Places of interest nearby

The New Forest is home to many rare species of snakes and lizards. To see them visit the **New Forest Reptile Centre** at Holidays Hill beside the A35 near Lyndhurst. It is open from April to September, 10 am to 4.30 pm.
☎ *02380 283141*

11 Rockford & Blashford Lake

The Alice Lisle

This is one of the loveliest walks in the whole New Forest area. Wessex Water have transformed the large gravel pits north of Ringwood into delightful lakes encircled by trees and dotted with islands. From the Alice Lisle pub at Rockford we follow the Avon Valley Path for part of our walk, taking a footpath beside Blashford Lake. Then we leave the Avon Valley Path to head east along a footpath running between Linbrook Lake and Northfield Lake. Our return route follows woodland paths to a quiet lane giving beautiful views over the Avon valley.

Distance – 4 miles.

OS Explorer OL22 New Forest. GR 161081.

Lakes and woods.

Starting point The Alice Lisle pub in Rockford.

How to get there The best approach is via the A338 Ringwood to Salisbury road. About 2 miles north of Ringwood turn for Moyles Court at Ellingham Cross along Ellingham Drove. When the road divides turn right, signed to Rockford and Linwood. Cross a bridge to a T-junction and turn right, signed to Rockford. The Alice Lisle is set back from the road on your right. Customers may leave their cars in the pub car park while they are walking.
Public transport: Wilts and Dorset bus service to Ellingham Cross (☎ 01202 673555 or 01722 336855). Follow the route along Ellingham Drove as described above. This will add 1¼ miles to the walk distance.

THE PUB

The delightful **Alice Lisle** pub is a real find, perfect for families with its spacious restaurant and large lakeside garden. But if you prefer to tuck yourself away there is a bar for the over eighteens and a special vintage garden for adults only. Dating back to the 17th century, the pub is named after a famous lady who lived nearby at Moyles Court. Although Alice Lisle was a Royalist she sheltered two wounded fugitives fleeing from James's army after Monmouth was defeated at the battle of Sedgemoor. For this humanitarian act she was condemned and executed. She used to visit a friend who lived at the house that is now our pub and I was told Alice's ghost haunts one of the bars, ringing mysterious bells at Christmas!

I am not surprised she is happy to revisit the pub as the

The New Forest

Looking towards Blashford Lake, near Rockford End.

service, food and drink are all excellent. Real ales are Ringwood Best, Gales HSB and Fuller's Best and London Pride. The menu is extensive and includes such dishes as whole grilled sea bass, Greek-style chicken breast stuffed with feta cheese marinated in herbs and wrapped in ham and 'Farmhouse Skillet' – minced beef and vegetables topped with cheese cooked in a cast iron skillet. The pub is very popular so I would advise booking beforehand in summer.

In summer opening times are from 11 am to 11 pm on Monday to Saturday and from 12 noon to 10.30 pm on Sunday. Food is served from 12 noon to 9 pm on Monday to Saturday and from 12 noon to 8 pm on Sunday. Contact the pub for winter times.
☎ *01425 474700*

1 From the **Alice Lisle** turn right along the Rockford road, cross the top of **Ivy Lane** and go through the small wooden gate by the **Avon Valley Path** sign.

2 Follow the path as it turns right and runs beside **Blashford Lake**, which sparkles through the trees on your left, with **Ivy Lane**

beyond the hedge on your right. The path curves left past the dinghy park for the **Spinnaker Sailing Club** then right along a gravel track to pass the clubhouse.

3 Turn left to go through a gate, still on the **Avon Valley Path**, and follow the footpath. The path curves left between **Blashford Lake** and **Snails Lake**.

4 Go through a gate and turn right for about 60 yards then turn left through an iron gate, following the **Avon Valley Path** sign. Keep ahead for about 200 yards to a narrow crossing path.

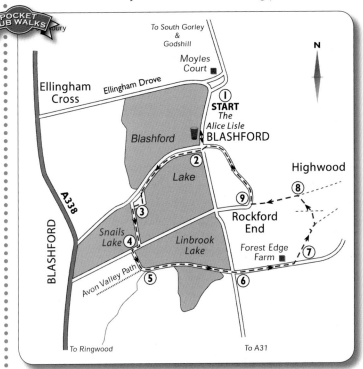

The New Forest

5 Leave the **Avon Valley Path** here and turn left to head east, with **Linbrook Lake** on your left, to go round a barrier to the corner of a road.

6 Turn right and then turn left up the lane marked with a 'No Through Road' sign for **Highwood**. The lane curves left past **Forest Edge Farm**. About 100 yards further on look carefully for a footpath sign on your left (difficult to see as it is hidden round the turning) indicating a track between two houses.

7 Turn left and follow the track as it climbs gently, tunnelling beneath hollies and oaks, past a small gate on the left. Follow the track round to the left and go through a gate. The track curves left and rises to run through light woodland. Go straight over a grassy crossing track to a wide gravel crosstrack. Turn left for a few yards to a gravelled T-junction.

8 Bear left along the gravel track, passing a grassy path on your left, and keep ahead over a cattle grid. The track runs downhill to the corner of a lane at **Rockford End**.

9 Turn right and follow this pleasant lane as it curves left downhill to join the Rockford road. Turn right and walk the few yards back to the **Alice Lisle**.

Places of interest nearby

Ringwood Town and Country Experience. Enjoy a unique and nostalgic trip into Ringwood's past and the surrounding area including vintage cars, old shops, a railway station and train and an RAF display. Gift shop and café. Open every day from Easter to October, 10 am – last admission 4.30 pm. From November to Easter it is open Sunday to Friday (not Saturdays), 10 am – last admission 3.30 pm.
☎ *01425 472746; website: www.rtce.co.uk*

12 **Hightown**

The Elm Tree

This is a very pleasant, easy ramble through attractive countryside west of the Avon close to Ringwood. Although it is a short walk there is a great deal of varied scenery to enjoy. From the Elm Tree pub we take the Crow road to join the track of the former railway that crossed the Forest from Brockenhurst to Wimborne Minster. At this point it runs close to Hightown Lake. Then we follow a tree-shaded footpath along the lake shore with beautiful views over the water before heading north along mainly woodland paths and returning to the Elm Tree across the fields.

The New Forest

Distance – 2½ miles.

OS Explorer OL22 New Forest. GR 163049.

Lake and views.

Starting point The Elm Tree pub.

How to get there Approach from the east along the A31. Turn left for Hightown and after about 2 miles you will see the thatched Elm Tree pub on your right. Approaching from Ringwood, turn south along the B3347, the Christchurch road. After about a mile turn left along the Hightown road, bearing right at the T-junction to the Elm Tree. Customers may leave their cars at the pub while they are walking.
Public transport: Wilts and Dorset buses (☎ 01202 673555 or 01722 336855).

THE PUB At the **Elm Tree** you can settle down in one of the comfortable armchairs or deep-padded window seats and be certain of a warm welcome and excellent food and drink. The bar and restaurant areas are spacious and inviting and it comes as no surprise that this is a real community pub welcoming many associations through its hospitable doors. The oldest part of the building was once a farm called The Elm Tree and is over four hundred years old with a huge fireplace and bread oven and heavily beamed ceiling.

You can choose from six real ales including Greene King and Ruddles brews. All the food is home-made, specialising in sea food and game, and sourced locally if possible. Among the choices might be Lymington crab salad, award winning sausages from Sway and rump of Dorset lamb. There is no excuse to go hungry at the Elm Tree! Dogs are welcome in the bar areas.

Opening times are from 11 am to 11 pm on Monday to Saturday and 12 noon to 10.30 pm on Sunday. Food is served from 12 noon to 3 pm and from 6 pm to 9 pm.
☎ *01425 472516*

1 Cross the road in front of the entrance to the pub's car park and take the Crow road, signed for **Burley** and **Bransgore**. Continue along the pavement for about ½ mile. Pass **Crow Arch Lane** on your right and a few yards further on you will see a bridleway sign on your left.

2 Turn left along the bridleway, which follows the track of the former railway. On your left you will catch glimpses of **Hightown Lake** through the bushes. After about ¼ mile you come to a small parking area on your right.

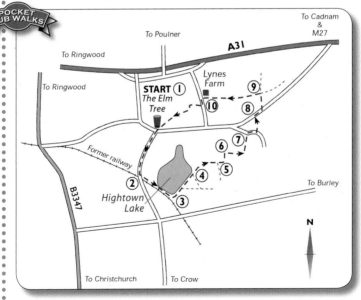

The New Forest

Hightown Lake.

3 Turn left to leave the track of the former railway and follow the lakeside footpath with a small stream on your right. Pass two footpath signs on your right. The path leads to a housing estate on your left and approaches a small gate. Do not go through the gate but turn right towards a stile with a yellow footpath sign.

4 Cross the stile and keep ahead, leaving a corrugated iron barn on your left, following a narrow path with a fence on your left and a stream on your right. Keep straight on past a footpath sign on your right to cross a plank bridge and a stile to a sharp left turn.

5 At this point the right of way has been altered and differs from the OS map. Follow the fenced path as it turns left then right to go through a gate to a wide gravel track.

6 Turn right for about 30 yards to the point where the track curves left. You are now back on the OS map. Keep to the track to pass a house on your right and continue between new fencing to an asphalt lane (not the Hightown road, which is over on your left).

7 Turn right for about 100 yards and as the lane curves right, turn left along a woodland path to meet the Hightown road.

8 Turn right beside the road for about 100 yards then turn left along a fenced gravel track to a crossing track.

9 Bear left and follow the track as it runs downhill past **Lynes Farm** to a lane.

10 Turn left for a few yards then turn right over a stile by a footpath sign. Keep straight on beside a field with a hedge on your left to cross another stile. Bear half-left over the grass to the next stile in the corner of the field. Cross a narrow plank bridge and keep ahead beside a field then aim across the next field towards the long thatched roof of the **Elm Tree**. Go round a barrier and the pub is on your right.

Places of interest nearby

Liberty's Raptor and Reptile Centre in Crow Lane, Ringwood offers fascinating flying displays with over 140 birds of prey including eagles, hawks and owls. The centre also houses 30 different species of reptile including a 15 ft Burmese python! Open from March to the end of October every day from 10 am – last entry 4 pm. During the winter months the centre is open at weekends only.
☎ 01425 476487; website: www.libertycentre.co.uk

13 Sway

The Hare and Hounds

Sway is a large village in the south of the Forest a few miles north of Lymington. It lies either side of the railway that was laid in 1886 to satisfy the demand for seaside holidays as the sleepy village of Bourne turned into the flourishing resort of Bournemouth. The previous railway line, running just south of Brockenhurst then west through Wimborne Minster to Poole, was dismantled and now makes a delightful walk, part of which we enjoy on this circuit. Other highlights include a ramble through one of the most beautiful woods in the Forest, Set Thorns Inclosure, and a visit to Sway's intriguing church.

The Hare and Hounds is a charming pub. An old coaching inn, it has been welcoming travellers for over two hundred years and can justly claim to be a pub 'where everyone's a local'. Long and low with several secluded areas and restaurants, there is plenty of room for families and those who prefer a quiet corner to eat their meal. Real ales are Timothy Taylor Landlord, Greene King IPA, Ringwood Best and a guest beer. The varied menu includes freshly prepared home-made specials such as liver and crispy bacon tower or chicken Hare and Hounds style – a chicken breast stuffed with mozzarella and spinach, wrapped in bacon and served with white wine sauce. There are interesting events throughout the year and barbecues where you can eat as much as you want! Dogs on leads are welcome in the bar and the large garden.

The pub is open from 11 am to 11 pm seven days a week throughout the year. Food is served from 12 noon to 9.30 pm.
☎ *01590 682404; website: www.harehounds.co.uk*

Distance – 5 miles.

OS Explorer OL22 New Forest. GR 283988.

Woodland and heathland paths and about a mile on the embankment of a dismantled railway.

Starting point The Hare and Hounds in Sway.

How to get there *The best approach is via Brockenhurst. Take the B3055, the Sway road, from the village centre. After about 1½ miles the road crosses the railway and the Hare and Hounds is about ¼ mile further on your left. Customers may leave their cars in the pub car park while they are walking.*
Public transport: Wilts and Dorset bus service to Sway (☎ 01202 673555 or 01722 336855). Or you can arrive by train (for train times and fares ☎ 08457 484950). The station is at point 2 of the walk.

The New Forest

1. Turn left from the front porch of the **Hare and Hounds** beside the B3055. At the crossroads turn right along **Church Lane**. You pass **Sway church** on your right and this delightful early Victorian building is well worth a visit. We discovered a great deal about Forest life in earlier days. It was consecrated in 1839 by Bishop Sumner who arrived on horseback. Continue to the junction and turn right up **Station Road**.

2. Pass the station on your left and at the fork bear left along **Mead End Road**. Leading straight ahead is **Brighton Road**, named after one of the gangs who came here to lay the railway. Pass **Normandy Close** on the right and continue up **Mead End Road**.

3. Turn right along **Adlams Lane**, passing an old house called **Kettlethorns** on the corner. This is a former smugglers' route and I read in the WI publication *It Happened in Hampshire* that a secret passage once used by smugglers connects Kettlethorns with the sea, presumably via safe houses along the way. The lane becomes gravelled as it leads downhill to a gate opposite **Set Thorns Inclosure**. Go through the gate and cross the grass directly ahead to go through another gate into this beautiful wood.

Long Slade Bottom.

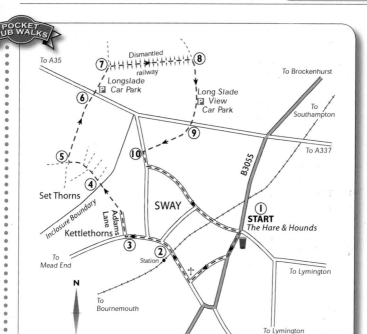

POCKET PUB WALKS

4 Pass a path immediately on your right and keep straight ahead up the gravel track, passing another path on your right. Continue straight ahead past a turning on your left and keep to your track to pass two tracks on the right and meet a broad gravel crosstrack.

5 Turn right along the track, which dips then rises. Keep ahead over all crossing tracks and go through the gate leading out of the inclosure.

6 Cross the minor road and walk straight ahead to the far end of **Longslade car park**. Pass the Forestry Commission barrier and follow the track leading down into **Long Slade Bottom** – worthy

The New Forest

of a prettier name! We see the valley very much as William Gilpin described it nearly 200 years ago, 'a beautiful valley … Arrayed in vivid green'.

7 When you reach the bridge supports of the dismantled railway, climb one of the gravel paths on either side and turn right along the wide embanked way ahead. A border of trees gives way at intervals to reveal splendid views over the valley on your left to the woods crowning **Hincheslea ridge**. Follow the way for almost a mile to the next bridge.

8 Before the bridge bear right to descend the embankment to a wide gravel track. Turn right to follow the track over the heath to **Long Slade View car park**. You will see the top of **Sway Tower** on the horizon. Built between 1879 and 1884 by Andrew Thomas Turton Peterson, it was one of the first buildings to be constructed in concrete without steel reinforcements. Cross the car park and the minor road.

9 Follow the right-hand of the two heathland paths ahead for about ¼ mile. The path dips into a shallow valley. Cross the dip and turn right to follow a broad green track to a road.

10 Turn left beside the road to go through a gate by a cattle grid then turn immediately left again along **Manchester Road**. Follow the road for about ¾ mile to meet the B3055 and return to the **Hare and Hounds pub**, which is almost opposite the junction.

Places of interest nearby

The old Forest port of Lymington has a fascinating story to tell and a visit to the **St Barbe Museum and Art Gallery** is well worthwhile.
☎ *01590 676969; website: www.stbarbe-museum.org.uk*

14 **By the Dark Water**

The Langley Tavern

In the south of the Forest the Beaulieu river tends to steal the limelight but to the east there is a stream just as appealing in its much quieter way, the Dark Water. Rising in the Forest it flows into the sea near Lepe and Stone Point. Our walks starts in Langley, an old village mentioned in the Domesday Book. We leave the village on a lane passing West Common to follow a branch of the Dark Water through a beautifully wooded valley. Footpaths through the oak and beech woods lead us to Exbury, famous for its wonderful garden. We return to Langley along a different route through more glorious woodland.

The New Forest

THE PUB The **Langley Tavern** is a big airy pub, family run, with a friendly atmosphere. There are two separate bars and children are welcome in the lounge bar and sunny conservatory. A delightful feature is the large garden fully equipped with a splendid play area for children and tables where the grown ups can enjoy a drink while keeping an eye on them! Ringwood ales are always on offer and three guest ales. A wide range of traditional pub food is available, with an excellent choice of 'specials'. On Sundays you can enjoy a tasty roast. As far as possible, the menus feature locally sourced produce. The Tavern is ideally situated close to the New Forest and the beach and overnight accommodation is available.

The bar is open from 11 am to 11.30 pm Mondays to Thursdays and Sundays; Fridays and Saturdays from 11 am to 12.30 am. Food is served on Tuesdays to Fridays from 11 am to 3 pm and from 6 pm to 10 pm. On Saturdays food is served from 11 am to 10 pm. The Sunday roast is served from 11 am to 4 pm. No food is available on Mondays. ☎ 02380 891402

The village of Exbury is visited on the walk.

Distance – 4 miles.

OS Explorer OL22 New Forest. GR 447010.

Woodland, streams, attractive village.

Starting point The Langley Tavern.

How to get there *The best approach is via the A326 Fawley road. Drive through Hardley and at the division take the right hand road for Lepe. Continue through Blackfield and Langley to the Langley Tavern on the right hand side of the road. Customers may leave their cars in the pub car park while they are walking.*
Public transport: The start of the walk can be reached by a Solent Blue Line bus (☎ 02380 618233).

1 Turn left from the **Langley Tavern** entrance and you will see a bridleway sign pointing down a tree-shaded path on your left. Turn left and follow the path to meet **West Common Road**. Turn left and continue past **Homer Farm Lane** and a caravan park to the point where the road divides.

2 Bear left along the lane and after a few yards you will see a footpath sign pointing down the lane. The lane runs downhill and becomes a grass and gravel track then a woodland path dipping into the **Dark Water valley**. Cross **Sturt Bridge** over the **Dark Water** and follow the beautiful path ahead through tangled woodland dotted with fine oaks and beeches. The lane becomes gravelled and leads beside high fencing on your right to meet the lane that continues north to cross **Blackwell Common** to **Blackfield**.

3 Turn right beside the lane for about 100 yards then turn left by a footpath sign to follow another delightful woodland path for

The New Forest

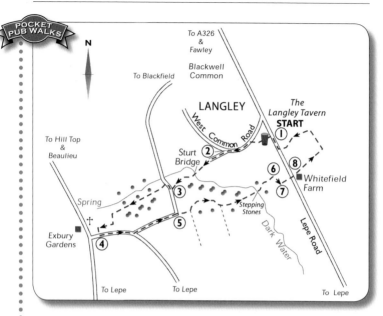

about ¾ mile. The path leaves the wood and curves left to run beside a hedge on your right and open grassland on your left before finally curving right between hedges to meet a lane in **Exbury village**. Turn left to walk the short distance to the road through the village.

4 To continue the walk we turn left but you may wish to explore the village first. If you would like to see the interesting church and visit **Exbury Gardens** turn right, then retrace your steps to follow the road heading east through the village. When the road divides take the left hand lane, signed to **Blackfield**, to rejoin the lane that crosses **Blackwell Common**. Follow the lane for about ¼ mile to the point where it curves sharply left.

5 On the corner you will see a footpath sign. Leave the road to follow the footpath and cross a stile by a gate. A grassy tree-

shaded path leads ahead between meadows. Keep to the same path as it curves left past a footpath on the right and weaves its way through remote woodland, bearing left past another joining footpath on the right. The path becomes a broad track bordered by hollies and the occasional grove of pine trees. Cross the stepping stones over the **Dark Water** (there is a handrail) and follow the narrow path ahead to cross a stile to paddocks. Keep ahead for only about 50 yards.

6 At this point our path turns rather unexpectedly right to lead over a stile and along the edge of a paddock to go over another stile.

7 Turn immediately left to walk between fences and cross a final stile to **Lepe Road**.

8 Across the road you will see yellow-brick **Whitefield Farm**. Cross the road and follow the tarmac track indicated by a footpath sign to the left of the farm. Pass the farm buildings and go through a gate. Keep ahead, then follow the track as it turns left. At this point the track becomes grassed over. Keep to the same track as it curves left again past a stile and footpath on the right and continue to return to **Lepe Road**. Turn right for the **Langley Tavern**.

Places of interest nearby

Exbury is famous for the spectacular 200 acre **woodland gardens** surrounding Exbury House, a neo-Georgian mansion now the home of Mr Edmund de Rothschild. The gardens are open from March to November and have a plant centre, gift shop and tea rooms.
☎ 02380 891203

15 Fawley & Ashlett Creek

The Falcon Hotel

The **south-eastern corner of the Forest**, with its wonderful views over Southampton Water and the Solent, may be dominated by the oil refinery but south of Fawley the countryside is still peaceful and beautiful. If you have any doubts let this walk convince you! Heath and meadow paths lead south from Fawley to bring you to a delightful lake carpeted with white waterlilies in summer. Then we head east to Ashlett Creek, an attractive inlet colourful with small boats, before crossing the fields to Fawley's historic church and returning to the village.

Distance – 5 miles.

OS Explorer OL22 New Forest. GR 459032.

Heathland, lake and views.

Starting point The Falcon Hotel, Fawley.

How to get there Follow the A326 south through Hardley and Holbury and at the division take the left hand road, the B3053, signed for Calshot. After about 1½ miles turn left, following the sign for Fawley village centre. Continue for about ¼ mile to the Square and the Falcon Hotel. Turn right into the hotel car park (available for customers while they are walking).
Public transport: Solent Blue Line runs buses to the Square (☎ 02380 618233).

THE PUB The **Falcon Hotel** has stood proudly overlooking the Square in this small village for over 160 years. During the 19th century it was the terminus for the Fawley Flyer, a horse-drawn coach that ran thrice weekly to Southampton. I was told that the first landlord of the hotel was killed by the Flyer and now his ghost calls in occasionally to keep an eye on things! I was not surprised as this welcoming pub is always a pleasure to visit, with two large bar areas offering plenty of room for everyone. The Falcon has a Cask Marque award for real ales. Ringwood ales are always available in addition to a guest ale. Delicious meals and bar snacks are served all day and include a daily roast with all the trimmings.

Comfortable overnight accommodation is available.

The Falcon Hotel is open for drinks and food all day from 11 am to 11.30 pm (12.30 am on Fridays).
☎ 02380 891005.

The New Forest

1 Turn right from the car park entrance to pass the front of the hotel on your right. Turn immediately right down a narrow lane signed 'The Lane, leading to Forge Lane'. Keep straight on between high hedges and cross the B3053 road.

2 Go through a gate and follow the wide track ahead over open grassland. Pass a footpath on the left and keep ahead along the main track to walk under some power cables. Go through a gate and continue with open heathland on your right. Approaching a crosstrack, bear a few yards left, then bear right to resume your original heading. The scene changes dramatically! On your

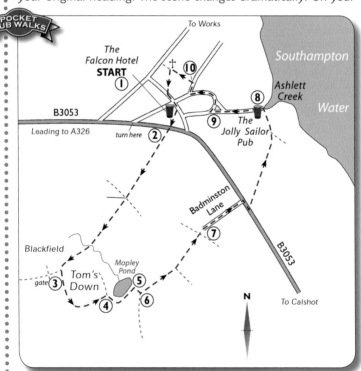

left hillsides thick with impenetrable gorse rise to woodland. The track dips through oak and beech woods to bridge a stream then goes up to run along a ridge of open heathland, **Tom's Down**, with the houses of **Blackfield** behind the trees on your right.

3 Navigate carefully here! You will see an iron gate about 30 yards ahead and a path over the heath on your left. Do not go as far as the gate but turn left to follow the heathland path heading south. After about 60 yards this divides. Take the right hand way. After about 200 yards the path curves left, heading a little to the right of **Calshot chimney**. Keep to the path as it curves again to head just to the left of the chimney.

4 The path meets a wide crosstrack. Turn right and go through a gate. Your path now runs downhill to a beautiful stretch of water known as **Mopley Pond**. It is so lovely it deserves to be called a lake! With the lake on your left, follow the track as it curves left past a house on the right.

5 Keep ahead through a gate and follow the woodland path ahead, which rises to a crossing track.

6 Turn left and keep straight ahead, with a fence at first on your right, over all crossing tracks. Follow the main gravel track uphill to cross the heath, heading a little to the right of **Calshot chimney** to a crosspath. Bear left. The chimney is now on your right. Keep ahead and go through a gate to **Badminston Lane**.

7 Follow the lane to cross the B3053. Turn right for about 20 yards then turn left along a wide grassy track to pass **Badminston Farm** on your right. The path narrows to approach a lane. Cross over and keep straight on along a narrow path burrowing through the trees. Go through a gate and walk down to an asphalt road. Bear left then go through a small wooden gate on your right. Follow the meadow paths to go through an iron gate and walk through

The New Forest

the trees to a crosspath. Turn left to **Ashlett Creek**. Pass the creek on your right.

8 Turn left up the road. You pass the **Jolly Sailor pub**, which serves full meals *(open 11 am to 11 pm on weekdays; Sundays 12 noon to 10.30 pm. Food is served from 12 noon to 2.30 pm and from 6 pm to 9 pm on Mondays to Fridays and from 12 noon to 9 pm at weekends)*. After about ¼ mile you will arrive at **Copythorne Lane** on your right.

9 Turn right to follow **Copythorne Lane**, which curves left to a road. Bear right past **Churchfields** and continue for a few yards to a red-topped 'No Through Road' sign and a footpath sign pointing left.

10 Turn left up a narrow footpath, which shortly becomes asphalt and runs beside a boarded fence on the left to grassland. Cross the grass, pass a footpath on the left and a few yards further on turn right into **Fawley churchyard**. Bear left to visit this beautiful church, which is one of the oldest in the Forest. After your visit turn left from the porch to retrace your steps to a division. Turn right through a small iron gate to walk past a children's playground on the left to go through a gate and cross the grass to a road. Turn left to return to **Fawley Square** and the **Falcon Hotel**.

Places of interest nearby

From Ashlett Creek you can follow a footpath along the coast leading south to **Calshot Marshes Nature Reserve**, important as a stopping-off point for migrating birds in spring and autumn. Winter visitors include avocet, arctic skua and snow bunting.